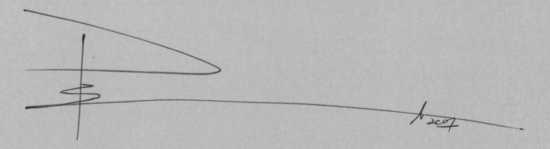

the aloha spirit

HAWAII

PETER LIK

It all started thousands of feet above sea level, flying around the cloudy peaks of the awesome Haleakala volcano. From that point, I knew I had to eternalize these stunning views on film.

The Hawaiian Islands feature some of the most ecologically diverse land masses on the planet. From the windswept sub-zero craters of Haleakala to the tropical paradise of the Pipiwai Trail, these beautiful islands span a wide spectrum of temperatures and landscapes. During my first ascent of Haleakala, I left the scorching heat of Lahaina in shorts and a T-shirt. Arriving at the summit, I found myself shivering cold and dizzy from altitude. Next time, I promised myself, I would wear warmer clothing!

The road which circumnavigates Maui is one of the most thrilling I have ever experienced. There are single lanes and switchbacks carved into vertical bluffs and breathtaking views at every turn. The sheer cliffs of Molokai are inaccessible by road, I hitched a ride with a helicopter to access some remote areas of the island. The rugged and utterly deserted coastline gave me the exhilarating impression I was discovering uncharted territory.

Hawaiians possess understated and graceful pride and are fiercely protective of the native cultural heritage. Every hilly outcrop and tumbling waterfall proudly bears a traditional name. I found many Hawaiian words difficult to pronounce and asking for directions became an art in itself. Following those directions was tougher still, resulting in some spectacular accidental discoveries.

In the end, all paths brought me to some of the most memorable photographs of my lifetime career. I am often quoted as saying "Mother Nature sets the scene... I simply capture it." The experience of photographing the Hawaiian scene has proven to be so completely fulfilling, that I cannot always find the right words to express myself. As usual, I am left to my photography to convey and express my feelings toward a truly unique landscape.

Following Page: Kapalua Bay, Maui

HAWAIIAN WAVES

Huge waves around the Seven Sacred Pools in Maui

placate the ocean's fury. The sheer power and energy

contained in each wave is an inspiring site. While many

surfers and water sport enthusiasts are eager to ride

these waves, my passion is to capture the truly beautiful

essence of Nature's strength. The enormity of these

waves defining the shoreline incites a truly remarkable

sensation of purity, energy, strength, and freedom.

Waikiki Palms, Oahu

Lanikai, Oahu

Following page: Kona Sunset, Big Island

BAMBOO

Dense bamboo forests inspire a sense of infinite splendor and possibilities. In the mist of the tall bamboo growths, there is a strong feeling of renewal radiating from the vivid green tones all around. The presence and energy of these natural wonders were surprisingly welcoming. I felt a powerful embrace from the surrounding bamboo and was compelled to capture this tremendous feeling.

Previous page: Pipiwai Trail, Hana, Maui

Venus Pools, Maui

Kauai

World famous surfer Andy Starn rips up a mega North Shore swell

Opposite page: Lahaina, Maui

Big Beach, Makena, Maui

HANA FALLS

There are many waterfalls along the "Road to Hana," an enchanting journey through the Island of Maui. Hana itself is a small, isolated town in Eastern Maui. The natural splendor of this area is accentuated by various botanical gardens. The picturesque and tranquil waterfalls, in and around Hana, serve as a perfect, peaceful retreat.

Pipiwai Stream, Maui

Following page: The painted forest on the road to Hana, Maui

KAPALUA

Along the west coast of Maui, Kapalua Bay features one of the finest beaches in Hawaii. The ebb and flow of the tides is mesmerizing. There is a seamless union between the Pacific Ocean and the beach, especially evident during the lazy evening hours. The sun sets the foreground rocks ablaze, presenting an adventurous and romantic view of stepping stones to the distant horizon.

Kamaole Beach, Maui

Baldwin Beach, Paia Coast, Maui

WAILELE

There are numerous graceful waterfalls throughout Hawaii, carving their own course down steep cliffs and through lush vegetation. This thick greenery enhances each view and beautifully frames Nature's ever-changing water sculptures.

Previous page: Waimoku Falls ,Pipiwai Trail, Maui

Rainforest church, Molokai

MOLOKAI

This gorgeous island is the least developed

of the eight main islands of Hawaii. Molokai

boasts tropical and exotic flora and fauna,

with the most common of these being

guava and eucalyptus. The South Shore

has many fish ponds while the eastern

half of the island is an elevated plateau.

The stunning terrain, pleasing climate and

tranquil settings are absolute perfection for

any visitor.

Rainforest meets the sea at Hamoa Beach, Maui

The dramatic head of Kahakuloa dominates the rocky coastline of West Maui

THE BIG ISLAND

Hawaii is the largest of the eight main Islands and is referred to as "the Big Island". Geographically it is the southernmost point of the United States. Like the other islands, the Big Island features striking botanical gardens brimming with tropical flora. Two active volcanoes on the Big Island, Kilauea and Mauna Loa provide both a sense of greatness and importance— a constant reminder of Nature's strength and vitality.

LANAI

Nicknamed "Pineapple Island" for its bountiful reserve

of the sweet fruit, Lanai has many natural wonders. Like

many of the other islands, Lanai has several botanical

gardens and alluring hiking trails. Perhaps this island is

best known for its various pristine, and secluded, white

sand beaches.

Honolua Bay, Maui

Oahu

KAUAI

Home to the magnificent Na Pali Coast State Park, the island of Kauai has numerous natural wonders to visit and explore. Wailua River and Hanalei Bay are both excellent locations to experience Kauai's true essence. Every trail that leads to one of these island's beaches is an adventure, a discovery of Nature's finest views and landscapes.

Na Pali Coast, Kauai

Honolua Bay, Maui

Opposite page: Molokai

Makapuu Beach, Oahu

Kaunakakai, Molokai

Lahaina, Maui

FLORA

The Vibrant colors of Hawaiian flora are known to represent the vibrant culture of the islands. Many people are familiar with the *lei* as a wreath of flowers that is draped around a person's neck upon arriving or leaving the islands, as a symbol of affection. Blooms and blossoms were everywhere

I was drawn to the flowers I photographed for their dynamic presence. There was something about these blossoms that was precious, yet not too delicate. The strength, beauty and tenderness of the Hawaiian spirit are clearly present in these magnificent flowers.

Jacarandas in bloom, Kula, Maui

KAHOOLAWE

The natural treasures of this location are particularly

enchanting. While Kahoolawe is the smallest of the

eight main islands, its charming setting delivers strong

character and abundant cultural presence. Comprised

of various small fishing communities, Kahoolawe is

also known as the center for forest restoration efforts.

Many areas of Kahoolawe are designated as spiritual

ancestral lands and are carefully guarded by locals.

Kilauea Volcano, Big Island

Silversword, Haleakala Crater, Maui

Kilauea, Big Island

Lahaina, Maui

RESTLESS WAVES

As the sun set on another perfect day, I witnessed a revelation. Waves raced toward me as I sat in the white sand, engrossed. Each rising and falling wave, if only for a moment, acted as a prism for the last rays of the sun. I ran into the water to get a better look. All the colors of the spectrum danced before me, surfing on the perfect waves. It was enchanting, playful and essential to the Hawaiian experience.

Previous page: Baby Beach, Maui
Na Pali Coast, Kauai

Hanalei Bay , Kauai

Following page: Koki Beach, Maui

Previous page: Makena Beach, Maui

Baby Beach, Lahaina, Maui

OAHU

Some of Oahu's greatest attractions include Waikiki Beach, Pearl Harbor, Diamond Head, and North Shore. Within the bounds of the state's capital, Honolulu, Waikiki Beach Walk is the home to one of the Peter Lik Galleries. As the most populous island, Oahu has the resources to accommodate heavy tourism. The development of this island continues to present each visitor with well groomed beaches and the idyllic vacation scene.

Wailua, Kauai

Huialoha Church, Kaupo, Maui

Previous page: Lumahai, Kauai

Slaughter Beach, Maui

Molokai Cliffs

Opposite page: Lanikai, Oahu

Following page: Kona, Big Island

Murphy Beach, Molokai

Previous page: Molokai

Hanalei Bay, Kauai

View of Waikiki and Diamond Head, Oahu

Maui

The constant flow of the ocean air moderates the tropical climate throughout Maui. Geographically, nearly half of Maui is positioned within five miles of the island's coastline. There is a massive range of tropical climatic conditions that satisfy the expectations of any visitor to the island. In the sun-drenched town of Lahaina, this art capital of Hawaii features one of the Peter Lik Galleries. Among the historical and picturesque buildings, the Peter Lik Gallery in Lahaina displays artwork that generously represents the spirit of Nature's Landscapes.

Front Street, Lahaina

WAIKIKI

While Waikiki is known as a center of the tourist industry,

there is a much more connected and spiritual side of the

area. The Waikiki shoreline is one of the most famous

beaches in the world, just one of the reasons people

have developed such an affinity for this part of Hawaii.

Once recognized as an essential vacation hot spot for

royalty, Waikiki beach has become accessible to many

visitors. It's a beautiful place to visit and experience a

vital element of the Hawaiian culture.

Peter Lik Gallery, Waikiki

PETER LIK MASTER PHOTOGRAPHER AIPP

As a completely self-taught artist, master photographer Peter Lik started his career in Australia and soon expanded his artistic vision worldwide. Huge panoramic photographs of landscapes showcase the brilliant colors and the elegant, spiritual terrain in Nature. These images speak for themselves and leave the casual viewer breathless; The truly conscientious observer will experience fine art.

Peter Lik is the most awarded photographer in history and remains a leader in fine art photography. His quest for the perfect shot never ends. He explores this world driven by a vigorous determination to express his vision of beauty and his profound respect for Nature. When you come to Peter Lik Galleries, you will interact with Peter's unique vision: a natural lifestyle accented with exotic high-end furniture and sculptures.

For those interested in purchasing, each fine art image is available in several different sizes to fit any space. Clients are able to choose the framing and liner for their piece. Aside from custom framing, Peter Lik Galleries also provides shipping worldwide.

Career: In 1984, after several years of experimenting with photography, Peter Lik was introduced to a large format panoramic camera.

He opened his first gallery in his hometown of Cairns. In a matter of months, several other galleries opened throughout Australia and the US. Since Peter's first visit to USA in 1989 he has been constantly drawn to the power of the American landscape. He has spent the last two decades exploring every state and national park, interpreting the landscape through his lens.

To display his unique vision of the American landscapes, he opened his first US gallery in Maui in 2003. Due to the success of this gallery and the huge response to Lik's art, he decided to go all the way and open 3 galleries in Las Vegas and one in Waikiki.

More recently, Peter opened a gallery in at The Plaza in NYC and another one in Miami, Florida. With Lik's passion, drive and unique style he is now recognized as the world's leading landscape photographer.

Photographic Awards

Australian Institute of Professional Photography

The prestigious Australian Institute of Professional Photography sets the benchmark for photographic excellence within Australia. Each year the peers of the industry judge the work of the premier professionals in the country. The AIPP has awarded Peter with their highest accolades, culminating in 2003 with his acceptance into an elite chapter as 'Master of Photography.' Becoming a Master can take many years and is an honour few Australian photographers achieve. Over the past five years Peter has received the recognition of the AIPP in the form of over thirty awards, including Silver, Silver with Distinction, and the coveted Gold. In 2002 in the competitive Landscape category, Peter's iconic image 'Ancient Spirit' earned the title of 'Highest Scoring Print' of the year.

2007

Australian Institute of Professional Photography Awards

Ghost...Silver with Distinction
Angel's Heart.................................Silver with Distinction
Heaven on Earth............................Silver
Icy Waters.......................................Silver

2006

PPA International Print Competition

Ghost...Merit
Angel's Heart.................................Merit
The Opera.......................................Merit

2005

Professional Photographers of America International Judging
114th Exhibition of Professional Photography

Ancient Spirit.................................2 Merits
Bamboo..Merit

2004

AIPP Nikon Queensland Professional Photography Awards

Bamboo..Silver
The Opera.......................................Silver

Australian Institute of Professional Photography Awards

The Opera..Silver with Distinction

Valley of the Shadows....................Silver

Spirits of Stone ....Silver

2003

AIPP Nikon Queensland Professional Photography Awards

Atlantic Reflections ....Gold

Shadowland ....Silver with Distinction

Stoneage...Silver

Paria Canyon.....................................Silver

Australian Institute of Professional Photography Awards

Atlantic Reflections ....Silver with Distinction

Paria Canyon.....................................Silver with Distinction

Shadowland ....Silver

Out There...Silver

2002

AIPP Nikon Queensland Professional Photography Awards

Ancient Spirit...................................Highest Scoring Landscape Print

Ancient Spirit...................................Silver

Australian Institute of Professional Photography Awards

Ancient Spirit...................................Silver with Distinction

Bodie Ghost Town...........................Silver with Distinction

Tranquility ....Silver

Fire Rock..Silver

2001

Australian Institute of Professional Photography Awards

Antelope Canyon ....Gold

Prince of Tides.................................Silver with Distinction

The Woolshed ....Silver

2000

AIPP Nikon Queensland Professional Photography Awards

The Jetty...Highest Scoring Color Print

The Jetty...Gold

Moonlight Head ....Silver

The Tanks..Silver

The Station..Silver

Australian Institute of Professional Photography Awards

The Jetty...Silver

Moonlight Head ....Silver

1999

AIPP Nikon Queensland Professional Photography Awards

Lone Shack..Silver

Australian Institute of Professional Photography Awards

Hopetoun Falls ....Silver with Distinction

Moonlight Head ....Silver

GALLERY LOCATIONS

UNITED STATES

NEW YORK

The Plaza Hotel
768 5th Avenue
New York, New York 10019

FLORIDA

Miami
701 Lincoln Road, Suite B
Miami Beach, Florida 33139

HAWAII

Maui
712 Front Street
Maui, Hawaii 96761
808 661 6623

Waikiki
Waikiki Beach Walk
226 Lewers Street #L118
Honolulu, Hawaii 96815
808 926 5656

LAS VEGAS

Venetian
#2071 Grand Canal Shoppes
3377 Las Vegas Blvd. South
Las Vegas, Nevada 89109
702 309 8777

Caesars Palace
T-10 Forum Shops
3500 Las Vegas Blvd. South
Las Vegas, Nevada 89109
702 836 3310

Mandalay Bay
#126 Mandalay Place
3930 Las Vegas Blvd. South
Las Vegas, Nevada 89119
702 309 9888

AUSTRALIA

Sydney
Level 2 QVB
455 George Street,
Sydney
NSW 2000 Australia
61 2 92690182

Noosa
Shop 2, Seahaven
9 Hastings Street,
Noosa Heads
QLD 4567 Australia
61 7 5474 8233

Port Douglas
19 Macrossan Street,
Port Douglas
QLD 4871 Australia
61 7 4099 6050

Cairns
4 Shields Street Cairns
QLD 4870 Australia
61 7 4031 8177

ORDERING ART WORK

Order by Phone

Our Fine Art Consultants are available to take your order seven days a week. If you have established a contact please make an effort to contact that person directly. You may call the Peter Lik Gallery you have visited by referring to the appropriate phone number listed on our gallery page. Please have your credit card and shipping information ready.

Gift Certificates

Our Gift Certificates are issued for any amount and may be used in any of our galleries.

Corporate Gifts

We can help you find the right products for your special events and employee recognition programs.

Limited Editions by Peter Lik

The Edition number on each image refers to the total number of photographs that will be printed. After all numbers of an edition are sold, that image will never again be printed as a photographic print, making your Limited Edition photograph a truly unique work of art.

Delivery

Both domestic and international shipping are available. Please allow 8-10 weeks for domestic shipping, and an additional 2-3 weeks for international deliveries. Our goal is to deliver framed images as early as possible. Turnaround time for unframed images is 2-4 weeks.

If you have a deadline to meet for a special occasion or gift, you may request a rush order for an additional cost.

Prices and Sales Tax

Peter Lik Galleries are all personally owned and operated by Mr. Peter Lik. Promotions are the same at all Peter Lik Galleries. We are required to collect sales tax in applicable states.

HAWAII THE ALOHA SPIRIT

PETER LIK

ART DIRECTION
John Villari

DESIGN
Thomas Proctor

COPY
Christina Madrid

PETERLIK.COM
888.545.6696

ISBN 978-0-9797927-0-0